BELWIN MASTER SOLOS

TRUMPET INTERMEDIATE

GRADED SOLOS for the Developing Musician
Edited by KEITH SNELL

Piano Accompaniment

CONTENTS

Solo Book available separately

Design: Odalis Soto

ORIENTATION

This book is one of three levels of trumpet solos in the Belwin Master Solos series. Prepared under the direction of Keith Snell, each of these folios contains a collection of graded solos that should prove to be a useful source for both the student and the teacher of the trumpet.

Each folio will contain works from a cross section of musical styles and historical periods as well as folk songs, traditional tunes and a selection of original compositions. For the student, these solos will provide material with specific challenges in rhythm, range, and key signatures in music that is both instructive and enjoyable to perform. The teacher will find these solos useful because each has been selected and arranged to challenge the student in different areas of technique and musicianship while providing exposure to a variety of musical styles that are enjoyable to perform.

INTERMEDIATE LEVEL - SOLOS

The solos in this folio are designed to provide the intermediate level trumpet student with challenges in all areas of the playing technique, including range, key signatures and complex rhythms, and in developing the technique of solo performance.

In an effort to expose the intermediate level student to a cross section of musical styles, arrangements of music from the various stylistic periods have been included. In order to accommodate the restrictions of key, meter and rhythm previously discussed, it has been necessary to make alterations to the original form of some of the pieces. This has permitted the use of a wider selection of music from the various historical and stylistic periods. It is hoped that this will help the intermediate level students to develop a greater understanding and appreciation for these musical styles and will encourage them to explore these styles further as their technique develops.

Trumpet Tune

Leopold Mozart (1719-1787)
Arranged by Derek Haydn

5

Nocturne

John Tyndall

7

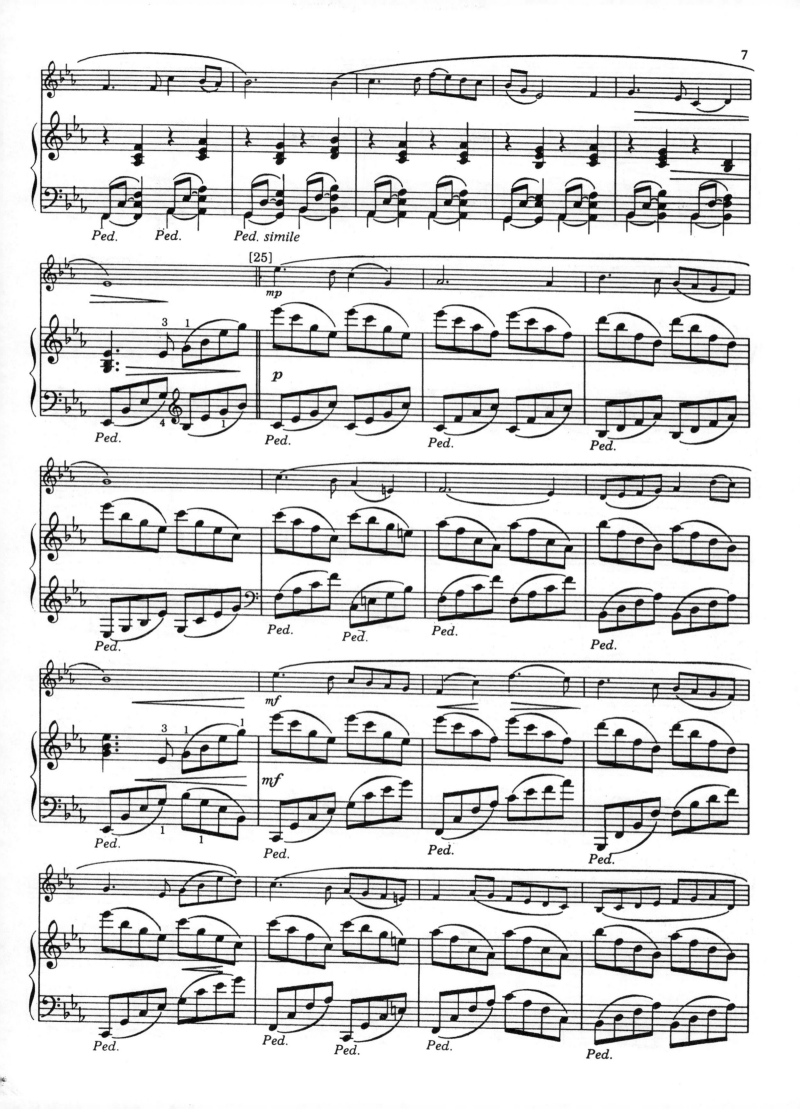

The Cuckoo

Swiss Folk Song
Arranged by Keith Snell

Briskly (detached)

12
[46]

Fanfare

Georg Phillipp Telemann (1681-1767)
Arranged by Keith Snell

"Air" from the Water Music

George F. Handel
Arranged by Derek Haydn

Let the Trumpets Sound!
from Cantata No. 207

Johann Sebastian Bach (1685-1750)
Arranged by Keith Snell

[85]

Polka Militaire

Christopher Nolan

Trumpet Tune
from "Heroic Music" for Trumpet

Georg Phillipp Telemann (1681-1767)
Arranged by Keith Snell

[33]

Rondo Capriccio

Keith Snell